Let Us Break Bread TOGETHER

A Passover Haggadah for Christians

PASTOR MICHAEL SMITH
RABBI RAMI SHAPIRO

PARACLETE PRESS
BREWSTER, MASSACHUSETTS

Copyright © 2005 by Michael A. Smith and Rami Shapiro

ISBN 0-7394-5011-5

Published by Paraclete Press
Brewster, Massachusetts

Printed in Mexico

Jesus said to his disciples,
"I have eagerly desired to eat this Passover with you . . ."

LUKE 22:15

TABLE OF CONTENTS

PREFACE

This small book is called a *haggadah*, Hebrew for "The Telling." It is the telling of the story of the Exodus of the Hebrew people from slavery in Egypt. The telling includes words and actions, using both mind and body to recall the horror of slavery and the joy of liberation. If you come to this haggadah at all familiar with the traditions of the Jewish Passover, you know that the bread of the title of this book refers to the unleavened bread, the matzah, that the Jews hurriedly baked in preparation for their exodus from Egypt. Breaking this matzah together has been a tribal and family ritual of the Jewish people for thousands of years. It is now finding its way into the homes and churches of Christians as well.

There are over two thousand versions of the Passover haggadah for Jews. This is not one of them. This is not a Jewish haggadah and is not meant for Jewish use. On the contrary, it is a Christian haggadah written explicitly for Christians in hopes of enriching their understanding of Passover.

For more and more churches and Christian families, the Passover seder (ritual Passover meal) is becoming a powerful opportunity to explore and honor the Jewishness of Jesus and the Jewish roots of Christianity. Yet the materials available to those Christians wishing to host a Passover seder are limited and often fail to explain the deeper meanings

of the seder from either the Jewish or Christian perspectives. This haggadah addresses that need. It grew out of Rabbi Rami's personal experience at a church *seder* in Murfreesboro, Tennessee, where he now lives. As Rabbi Rami puts it:

> I was impressed by the sincerity of the participants but saddened at the inability of their haggadah to adequately explain Passover and to engage them in a manner that honored the Jewish faith and yet spoke directly to their faith as Christians. They did their best to follow the Jewish seder rituals but could not make them their own. I felt a need to help them understand Passover on a deeper level, and I knew this could best be done by creating a haggadah specifically addressed to Christians. Not being a Christian myself, I turned to my friend Mike Smith, pastor of the First Baptist Church of Murfreesboro. I felt certain we could collaborate to create a haggadah that would help Christians experience an authentic and meaningful Passover seder.

The haggadah you are reading is the result of that collaboration. We have labored in the context of friendship and mutual respect. Both of us are steeped in our respective religious traditions. We have no desire to blur the distinctions between those traditions or even to try to create a haggadah that might be used by both faiths. This is a Christian haggadah intended for use by Christians in their homes and churches.

In addition to its intended audience, another unique feature of our haggadah is that it follows a question-and-answer format. We chose this format for several reasons. First, asking questions is at the heart of both Judaism in general and the Jewish seder in particular. Second, asking and answering questions can serve as a catalyst for conversation among participants on the major themes of Passover: slavery, freedom, and one's personal relationship with God. Third, the format maximizes the opportunity for guests to participate in the seder. While there are sections of the haggadah designated for the LEADER and others for the

COMMUNITY as a whole, most of this haggadah is read by going around the table or room and inviting people to read the questions and answers in turn.

We hope that your participation will not end with the reading of the haggadah and that the questions wrestled with during the reading of the haggadah will set the tone for table discussion during the meal. While it is natural to engage in small talk, the seder is best experienced as an opportunity to seriously explore the reality of slavery and liberation in your life.

We have done our best to create a haggadah that honors the teachings of both Judaism and Christianity. Some in each of our faith traditions may conclude that we have failed, ought not to have undertaken such a task, or have created something a little dangerous. We feel the potential benefits outweigh the risks. As more and more Christians take on the Passover seder as part of their religious life, it will benefit everyone to do so not as an experience of the exotic, but as a way of enriching understanding and appreciation of Judaism even as Christians deepen their connection to Jesus.

Serious Jews and Christians have much to learn from one another. We do not have to become like one another in practice or belief to do so. In fact, exposure to our differences may help us grow in faith and understanding.

We hope our haggadah proves useful to individuals, families, and churches. Please feel free to adapt the haggadah as you see fit. We regard it as a task begun, not finished, and would welcome suggestions from our readers on how it might be improved.

May both faith and freedom deepen in your life.

Mike Smith, Pastor, First Baptist Church, Murfreesboro, Tennessee
Rami Shapiro, Rabbi, One River Foundation

ACKNOWLEDGMENTS

We might never have met except through the efforts of Jeff and Judy Fryer. They brought us together over meals, setting the stage for further conversations and a deepening friendship. Good introductions expand the circle of fellowship and make the world a better place. We would be remiss if we failed to take this opportunity to thank Jeff and Judy for their ministry of introduction.

Our thanks also go to the staff of Bangkok Café, a small Thai restaurant one block off the town square. Not only do they prepare excellent food, they also consistently provide a quiet, unrushed environment in which a Jewish rabbi and a Christian pastor can take the time to get to know one another. To find such an oasis of calm is a great blessing, and we are grateful.

Neither of us can begin to name all the teachers, writers, synagogue and church members, and mentors who have influenced us. Suffice it to say both of us have had the privilege of being influenced by men and women who consistently sought to foster meaningful dialogue between those of various faith traditions. They, of course, are not responsible for any errors of fact or perspective that may have crept into our work. Still, we probably would not have become the kind of persons who would listen well to one another without their influence.

Both of us have the good fortune to be sustained by spouses who encourage us in our work. We take this opportunity to thank them for their support and love.

A NOTE ON TRANSLATION

We quote from the Hebrew Scriptures, the Greek New Testament, and the Hebrew text of the traditional Jewish haggadah. Our English translations of the Greek come from both the New Revised Standard Version and the New International Version of the Bible. Our English translations of the Hebrew are Rabbi Rami's.

Translation is more art than science, and you might want to compare our renderings to other versions. Rabbi Rami's translations are intended to highlight the spiritual message of the Hebrew, and in this way to make the meaning of the text as clear as possible.

The one area in which we departed from conventional translations is the traditional Hebrew blessings over various foods. The Hebrew reads *Baruch Ata Adonai Eloheinu Melech haOlam* and is literally translated as *Blessed are you, Lord our God, sovereign of the universe.* . . .We have translated the formal *Lord our God* to *Abba*, Hebrew for "Father," a term better reflecting Jesus' understanding of his and our relationship with God.

Remember that Hebrew is read from right to left, rather than from left to right. This order is reversed in both the transliteration and, of course, in the English translations.

A NOTE TO THE LEADER

Coordinating a Passover seder is a big job! You are responsible for pulling together invitations, setup, food preparation and the reading of the haggadah. We have tried to make leading the seder as easy as possible. Even so, you may want to secure extra help with at least two parts of the seder experience.

The first of these is the invitation. If your church or family is used to holding a Passover seder, you may not need our advice, but if seder is a new practice for you and your community, we suggest you send a brief letter of explanation along with the formal invitation. The letter should highlight the following matters.

The Jewishness of Jesus

The centrality of the Passover seder in the life of Jews and, therefore, Jesus as a Jew

The universal application of the Passover message: liberation from the various slaveries that constrict our lives

The healing power that comes from sharing a sacred meal with family and friends

In addition to the letter and formal invitation, we think it wise to prepare your guests in two other ways as well.

First, encourage them to bring canned goods for donation to a soup kitchen or homeless shelter. The seder includes a specific time to mention such gifts of food, and you don't want people to feel left out because they did not know to bring a food donation. Second, the seder ends with children hunting for the *afikomen*, a broken piece of *matzah* hidden earlier in the service that, once found, represents healing and wholeness. The finder is rewarded with a gift. The gift should be monetary, and the money should then be donated to a cause of the child's choosing. To ensure that the children understand where their prize will go, you may want to explain that part of the seder in your letter of invitation and ask parents to discuss the matter in advance with their children. Parents of the child who finds the afikomen can then tell you where to send the donation. You should probably prepare a short list of possible recipients as well and include this along with your invitation.

THE CHRISTIAN-PASSOVER CONNECTION

Because Jesus was an observant Jew, Passover was a central part of his life. The Gospel According to Luke makes it very clear that Jesus celebrated Passover as a child: "Now every year his (Jesus') parents went to Jerusalem for the festival of the Passover" (Lk. 2:41). It also tells us that at the age of twelve Jesus caused his parents some worry: "When the festival was ended and they started to return, the boy Jesus stayed behind in Jerusalem, but his parents did not know it" (Lk. 2:43).

As in his early days, Passover played an important role in the life of Jesus in his last days.

> Then came the day of Unleavened Bread, on which the Passover lamb had to be sacrificed. So Jesus sent Peter and John, saying, "Go and prepare the Passover meal for us that we may eat it." They asked him, "Where do you want us to make preparations for it?" "Listen," he said to them, "when you have entered the city, a man carrying a jar of water will meet you; follow him into the house he enters and say to the owner of the house, 'The teacher asks you, "Where is the guest room, where I may eat the Passover with my disciples?"'" He

will show you a large room upstairs, already furnished. Make preparations for us there." So they went and found everything as he had told them; and they prepared the Passover meal. (Lk. 22:7–13)

Jesus said to his disciples, "I have eagerly desired to eat this Passover with you before I suffer" (Lk. 22:15). *This Passover* refers to the seder; *with you* refers to all his disciples past and present. Observing the Passover seder is a way of continuing to honor this fervent wish of Jesus.

Jesus used this, his final Passover seder, as an opportunity to teach. During the seder Jesus asked his followers to "[d]o this in remembrance of me" (Lk. 22:19). While today we may interpret Jesus' words differently, the early church took him to be referring to the Passover seder, and made the seder central to Christianity for the next three hundred years.

There are other connections between Passover and the Church. Luke's Acts of the Apostles makes two references to the Festival of Unleavened Bread (Acts 12:3; 20:6), which is another name for the Jewish holy day of Passover. These passages link Peter and Paul to Passover services in Jerusalem and Greece, respectively.

The order of the Passover meal is the basis for the early church's Lord's Day worship called the Agape Feast and Eucharist. After the year 300 CE, the Agape Feast was separated from the Eucharist, and five Church Councils between 320 CE and 816 CE sought, albeit unsuccessfully, to eliminate the Agape Feast altogether. The Feast is still celebrated in the Greek Orthodox Church and in some denominations of Protestant Christianity as well.

Today, some seventeen hundred years later, renewed interest in the Jewishness of Jesus has led many Christians to reclaim the Passover seder as part of their heritage. Christian and Jewish seders, however, differ from one another. For Christians the Passover seder connects them to

Jesus the Jew and thus deepens their understanding of Jesus the Christ. For Jews the Passover seder is a global family reunion focusing on the retelling of the core story of the Jewish people: their liberation from slavery in Egypt. The Passover story is the key to Jewish self-understanding, leading as it does to receiving the revelation of God's Torah (the Five Books of Moses) at Mount Sinai, the confederation of the Hebrew tribes into a single people, and the ultimate settling of that people in the Promised Land of Israel.

While borrowing heavily from the original seder of the Jews, this Christian haggadah does not pretend to be in any way Jewish. Participants in this seder are not imitating the Jews, but learning from them.

It is the belief of both Dr. Smith and Rabbi Rami that by deepening our respective faiths and our understanding of each other's faith we will come to a common ground of respect for both the differences between us and the greater unity that surrounds us. We hope this haggadah contributes a bit to finding that common ground.

SETTING THE SEDER TABLE

The seder is a ritual meal and requires some formal preparation. Here are the items you will need and how to make them.

The Seder Plate. Because you may be new to hosting or leading a seder, we have paid special attention to the setup of the seder plate, a central part of the service itself.

The actual plate itself may be as simple as a paper plate or as fancy as a special seder plate purchased at a Judaica gift shop. If you plan to host an annual seder in your home you may prefer to purchase a plate especially designed for seder use. You can do this on-line or through a local synagogue gift shop. The advantage of the plate dedicated for the seder is both aesthetic and spiritual. Aesthetically such a plate can add to the special atmosphere of your seder table; spiritually it can make the nonverbal statement that this isn't an ordinary meal, but a holy feast.

If you are hosting a large gathering, purchasing such plates is not practical, though you may opt to have one for the leader's table. Strong paper or plastic plates will do just fine, and it is a good idea to have one at each table so that people can see what the seder is referring to as the service makes reference to each item on the plate. If yours is a church seder, you might ask the children in your church school to decorate plates that will be used at the community seder. Teachers can use this exercise as an opportunity to talk about Passover and the seder, and to explain the different symbols to the students in advance of the meal. Regardless of the kind of plate you use, the plate itself will hold six items:

Charoset. *Charoset* is a mixture of apples, nuts, red wine or grape juice, and spices, and symbolizes the mortar the Jewish slaves made in their building pyramids for Pharaoh. To make charoset, you will need 1 cup of walnuts, 1 Granny Smith green apple, 2 tsp. cinnamon, 2 tsp. sugar (optional), and red wine or grape juice to moisten. Chop the nuts and apples to the consistency you want. Mix in the spices, and moisten with wine or grape juice. The texture of the charoset should remind you of mortar, so do not make it smooth or buttery.

Zeroa. *Zeroa* is a roasted shank bone of a lamb or neck of a chicken. Zeroa is symbolic of the Paschal lamb offered as the Passover sacrifice in Temple days. From a Christian perspective it is symbolic of Jesus, "For Christ, our Passover lamb, has been sacrificed for us," (1 Cor. 5:7 NIV). You can purchase a shank bone or chicken neck at most butcher shops. Wrap the shank bone in foil and roast it in the oven for about thirty minutes. Zeroa is a symbol only and is not eaten during the Passover meal.

Baytza. *Baytza* is an egg, first hard-boiled and then roasted. The hard-boiled egg was a reminder of the festival sacrifice held at the Temple in Jerusalem. With the destruction of the Temple (first by the Babylonians in 586 BCE and later by the Romans in 70 CE), the Jews began to associate the hard-boiled egg with mourning the loss of their Temple. Today the egg reminds all of us to mourn the suffering of all peoples trapped in the horrors of slavery.

Karpas. *Karpas* is a green vegetable, usually parsley, and represents the reemergence of life at springtime. During the seder the karpas is dipped in saltwater and eaten, so make sure you have a small sprig of parsley for each guest. The saltwater represents the tears of suffering that become tears of joy when we move from slavery to freedom.

Maror. *Maror* is bitter herbs, usually horseradish root or prepared horseradish. Maror represents the bitterness of life lived under slavery. You can buy prepared horseradish at most grocery stores.

Saltwater. In addition to these food items, the seder plate holds a small dish of saltwater in which the *karpas*/parsley is dipped. If your plate can't hold the saltwater, a separate dish is fine.

While preparing the seder plate is not a huge ordeal, it may take an hour. It is wise to prepare the plate in advance. Allowing children to help is another fun way to get them involved in learning about Passover and in feeling some investment in the success of the meal.

As you prepare each item invite the children to talk about slavery. You may choose to focus on ways in which they are trapped and enslaved. Slavery is not something that younger children understand right away. Talk with them about habits they cannot seem to break. Older children can explore how they can get enslaved to feelings and expectations, and how our consumer society tries to enslave them to certain brands and logos. Make sure to talk about ways they can maintain their freedom from such slavery.

Matzah. *Matzah* does not go on the seder plate itself. You can purchase a special three-tiered matzah plate to hold the three pieces of matzah needed for the seder. Any plate wide enough to hold the matzah will do, however. While the seder requires three pieces of matzah, have extra matzah on hand since lots of matzah may be consumed during the meal. A separate plate provided to hold the three pieces of matzah used in the seder is covered by a cloth or napkin.

Matzah is the unleavened bread that the Israelites took with them when they escaped from Egypt. The Bible tells us that the people had no time to bake leavened bread, and had to settle for matzah instead. It is also true that matzah is lighter than bread, easier to carry, and lasts longer then regular bread.

If you go to your local supermarket to purchase matzah for your seder you may notice that some boxes will say the matzah inside is kosher for Passover, while some boxes will say the matzah is not kosher for Passover. *Kosher* is the Hebrew word for "fit." Matzah is fit for Passover only if the grain used to make the matzah has been protected from dampness prior to baking, and baked in a hurry (about eighteen minutes). The concern here is that the dough used for the matzah, if allowed to dampen will produce yeast or leaven, and leavened products are prohibited to Jews during the week of Passover.

The Hebrew word for leavened products is *chumetz,* and Jews observing Passover abstain from eating anything that contains chumetz. In addition they remove all leavened products from their homes. The idea is to spend one week leaven-free. Why? Because leavened breads were made with sour dough, chumetz came to represent all the things we do that bring slavery and sourness into our lives and the lives of those with whom we come into contact. Avoiding chumetz is a challenge to weed out sourness and enslavement during the Passover week, and to stop living soured and enslaved lives. This is a challenge all of us can appreciate and make our own.

As a Christian you may choose not to concern yourself with the details of kosher and unkosher matzah, and while you may choose to eat chumetz during Passover, and even at your seder, the presence of matzah is still a reminder of the deeper work of this holy week. As Jesus taught, "[I]t is not what goes into the mouth that defiles a person, but it is what comes out of the mouth that defiles" (Mt. 15:11).

In addition to the matzah eaten at the seder it is customary to eat soup with matzah balls. To make matzah balls you need 4 eggs, 1 cup of matzah meal, and a pinch of salt. Beat the egg yolks and salt together. Beat the egg whites separately until they are very stiff. Fold the egg yolks and egg whites together, and add the matzah meal. Roll the mixture into balls and drop them into rapidly boiling salted water in a very large pot. Boil for forty-five minutes with the pot covered.

The Afikomen. Another aspect of the seder you may choose to prepare in advance is the *afikomen*, or "dessert." We mentioned earlier that this was a piece of matzah hidden during the service and sought out by the children toward the end of the meal. Technically the seder cannot be concluded without eating the afikomen.

During the seder the middle of the three pieces of matzot is broken in half and the smaller half is hidden away. The challenge to you as leader is this: if the children know the afikomen is to be hidden, and that they will be asked to find it, and that there is a prize for doing so, they will never take their eyes off of you, making it very difficult for you to hide the afikomen. Here are two ways to get around this.

First, you could hide the afikomen in advance of the meal. While technically incorrect, it does solve the problem. Second, you can ask another adult to do the hiding on your behalf. While the children are focused on you, your surrogate can hide the afikomen undetected. Whoever hides the afikomen should make sure it can be found, but not too easily. If you have lots of children at your seder you may wish to hide more than one piece of matzah.

A word about wine. It is traditional to drink four cups of wine during a Passover seder. Grape juice is a fine substitute for those for whom wine is inappropriate. Make sure you have enough of one or the other for the entire seder.

Elijah's Cup. In addition to the four cups of wine or grape juice that you will drink at your seder, there is a fifth cup, filled only at the conclusion of the seder. This cup is called *Kos Eliyahu*, or Elijah's Cup. Judaism teaches that Elijah, who is called the Prophet of Peace, will come to announce the coming of the Messiah. Jesus, too, makes reference to Elijah. His disciples ask him, "Why do the scribes say that Elijah must come first [before the Messiah]?" Jesus said to them, "Elijah is indeed coming first to restore all things" (Mk. 9:11-12). Toward the conclusion of the seder Elijah's Cup is filled and the doors to the home or church are opened to allow the spirit of Elijah to enter. Elijah makes his presence known by taking a sip of wine from the *Kos Eliyahu*.

There need be only one Elijah's Cup at your seder, most likely placed at the table of the seder leader. When the Cup is filled and the doors are opened, invite the children to gather around the Cup to see if Elijah does in fact take a sip. You might invite the youngest children to drink a bit from the Cup as well to honor Elijah's visit and thus ensuring that the wine or grape juice in the Cup does indeed decrease.

A pillow. It is customary for the leader to recline on a pillow during the seder as a sign that this is a meal of free and fearless people. The pillow is referenced during the seder and you may wish to have a small one on hand to symbolize the free nature of this gathering.

THE SEDER

LEADER'S WELCOME

LEADER

"How very good and pleasant it is when kindred live together in unity." (Ps. 133:1)

Tonight we sit in special fellowship, honoring each other and God with a Passover meal. We do so for at least three reasons. First, Jesus celebrated Passover, and our Passover links us to him and to the ancient Jewish roots of our own faith. Second, the celebration of freedom, which is at the heart of Passover, is universal, inspiring people of different faiths and even people aligned with no faith to labor for liberation. Third, the personal challenge of Passover—freeing ourselves from personal enslavements of thought, word, and deed—may benefit all of us.

If we are to benefit from our Passover seder, however, we must be authentic in what we are doing. We must not simply imitate the Passover of our Jewish neighbors. Instead we must engage in our own spiritual liberation. Our seder, therefore, is not an imitation but an adaptation. We draw from Judaism but we do not pretend to be Jews. In this way, we may learn from our deepest historical roots yet remain true to ourselves and our faith.

Our meal is called a *seder*, from the Hebrew term for "order." The Book of Genesis tells us that God orders all creation. Though we affirm this is so, we must confess we often cannot sense God's ordering presence. Our own habit of trying to control things for ourselves gets in the way. Paradoxically, the more we seek to control things, the more they spin out of control.

The story we tell on Passover is one of human control and divine liberation. Egypt symbolizes our enslavement to power, the kind of bondage that results from our seeking to control our own lives. Pharaoh symbolizes our addiction to power and to the need to control. The Jewish people symbolize all of us who are enslaved in some fashion to the ego's need to control. The entire Passover meal is a celebration of our rediscovery of God's order and the liberation that comes when we refocus our attention on the only thing we can control: our decision to surrender control of our lives to God.

To that end let us pray: O Lord of all creation and of each human life, hear now our prayer. As we gather about this table, relive the story of the Exodus, and partake of the food provided, we ask that you use the occasion toward your ends. May our felt need for you be deepened, our bonds with one another be tightened, our willingness to surrender to your rule be strengthened, and our ministry to others be extended. Amen.

CANDLE LIGHTING

[*Each table should have two white candles that are lighted for Passover.*]

LEADER

"Let your light shine before others, so that they may see your good works and give glory to your Father in heaven" (Mt. 5:16).

LEADER

We begin our seder with the making of light. Yet light makes sense only in contrast to darkness. Take a moment to recall and embrace the dark times of your life: times of confusion, depression, and loss. Allow yourself to feel the "Dark Night of the Soul" not as punishment for sin but as prelude to salvation: "there was evening, there was morning, a first day" (Gen. 1:5).

[*The candles are lighted while the participants' eyes are closed.*]

Now open your eyes and behold the light as a gift from the One who says "Light" and light comes into being.

COMMUNITY

בָּרוּךְ אַתָּה יְיָ, אֱלֹהֵינוּ מֶלֶךְ הָעוֹלָם,
אֲשֶׁר קִדְּשָׁנוּ בְּמִצְוֹתָיו
וְצִוָּנוּ לְהַדְלִיק נֵר שֶׁל יוֹם טוֹב:

Baruch Ata Adonai Eloheinu melech haolam, asher kidshanu b'mitzvotav v'tzivanu l'hadleek nair shel yom tov.

Bless you, Abba, Sovereign of all life, who honors us with the opportunity to kindle the light of freedom.

QUESTION

What does it mean to be free? Is freedom simply a matter of doing what we wish whenever we wish?

ANSWER

There is a difference between independence and freedom. As a child matures she learns to say no to the will of others. This is the beginning of her independence. As she grows she adds to this no a yes affirming her desires and will. Many of us never mature beyond this point. We call this freedom, but it is only independence. True freedom comes when we can also say no to our own desires and yes to the needs and desires of others. True freedom arises not when we do our will but when we do God's will: doing justly, acting compassionately, and walking humbly (Mic. 6:8).

THE SYMBOLS OF PASSOVER

LEADER
To help us understand the meaning of our seder as a whole, we explore the meaning of each part.

QUESTION
What is the meaning of the roasted shank bone?

ANSWER
The shank bone, called *zeroa*, reminds us of the Paschal lamb offered to God by the Jews. For us Christians it calls to mind the significance of Jesus, whom we remember as God's Paschal Lamb offered on our behalf.

QUESTION
What is the meaning of the boiled egg?

ANSWER
For many Jews and Christians the egg, *baytza* in Hebrew, symbolizes the circle of life and death and the turning of the seasons. Passover, like Easter, is a spring holy day. In the Jewish tradition, Passover marks the renewal of life in the natural world. Christians inevitably are reminded of the resurrection of Jesus. In Judaism the egg is also considered a sign of mourning, reminding us to honor the suffering of those trapped in slavery, both the enslaved and the enslavers, and, as Christians, to honor the Passion of our Lord whose suffering was the key to our liberation.

QUESTION

What is the meaning of the bitter herbs?

ANSWER

The herbs are called *maror*, "bitter," and are eaten to remind us of the bitter taste of slavery in all its forms.

QUESTION

What is the meaning of the mixture of nuts, apples, and spices?

ANSWER

This is *charoset* and symbolizes the mortar the Hebrew slaves used to build the pyramids of Egypt. It reminds us all of the great yet ultimately futile works to which so many individuals and societies are enslaved.

QUESTION

What is the meaning of the parsley on our seder plate?

ANSWER

This is called *karpas* and represents hope. Later in our seder we will dip the karpas in saltwater, symbolizing the sadness of slavery, the joy of liberation, and the effort needed to move from the first to the second. Hope must lead to action if our desire for liberation is to become the reality of freedom.

QUESTION

What is the meaning of the unleavened bread?

ANSWER

Matzah has many meanings. It is called the "Bread of Affliction", reminding us when we eat it of the suffering of the poor. It is flat to remind us not to become puffed up but instead to remain simple and humble. It is dry to remind us that we cannot live by bread alone, that we need the Water of Life that is God. Matzah for Passover is prepared under strict supervision of rabbis whose job is to make sure the dough does not sour and rise. For this reason when we eat matzah we are reminded to root out the sourness in our lives and the sourness we bring to the lives of others.

QUESTION

Why are there three *matzot* on the table?

ANSWER

The number three is sacred in both Judaism and Christianity. In Judaism it may represent the three pillars of Judaism: God, Torah, and Israel; the three pillars of civilization: revelation, divine worship, and acts of loving kindness; and thought, word, and deed—what Judaism refers to as the "Three Garments of the Soul"—the three primary ways we engage each other and the world. For Christians, the three matzot may symbolize the completeness of God's saving work: the calling out of God's special people, the extension of God's grace to the Gentiles, and the promise of a new heaven and earth in which God's people will dwell. The number is also special to Christians as a representation of the three persons of the Trinity: God the Father, God the Son, and God the Holy Spirit.

QUESTION

Why is so much wine or grape juice needed?

ANSWER

It is traditional for guests to drink four cups of wine or grape juice at a seder. The number four reminds us of four aspects of liberation mentioned by God in Exodus 6:6-7: "I shall take you from under your burdens"; "I shall rescue you"; "I shall redeem you"; and "I shall take you unto myself."

QUESTION

How might we understand "I shall take you from under your burdens"?

ANSWER

Some burdens are so heavy as to leave us feeling crushed. We cannot push them away. Only God can snatch us safely from beneath such burdens.

QUESTION

How might we understand "I shall rescue you"?

ANSWER

Our attachments are sometimes so strong we cannot pull ourselves loose. It is then that we must await God's rescue, allowing his power to replace our own.

QUESTION

How might we understand "I shall redeem you"?

ANSWER

Our enslavement to wrongful habits robs us of joy and hope. We cannot redeem ourselves because it is to ourselves that we are enslaved. Only God can redeem us and free us from captivity.

QUESTION

How might we understand "I shall take you unto myself"?

ANSWER

Our primary enslavement is to self and selfishness. True freedom comes when we surrender our small self to God and allow God to take us into his far greater Self.

QUESTION

What is the purpose of the extra empty wine cup?

ANSWER

This is call *Kos Eliyahu*, the Cup of the Prophet Elijah. The Bible tells us that Elijah never died, but was taken directly to heaven. Jewish tradition says Elijah returns to earth regularly to help people in need. On Passover it is said he visits every seder and shares a bit of drink with the guests to remind us that God never abandons us. Elijah is also the Prophet of Peace who will herald the coming of the Messiah. For Jews this will be seen as the first coming of the Messiah; for Christians it will be seen as the second coming. Offering a place at our table for Elijah reminds us to offer a place in our hearts for redemption.

QUESTION
What is the meaning of the saltwater?

ANSWER
The saltwater has three meanings. First, it represents the tears of sadness that are shed in slavery. Second, it symbolizes the tears of joy that flow at the moment of liberation. Third, it reminds us of the effort and sweat that go into moving from the first to the second.

LEADER
There is a great deal to remember about our Passover seder. Our hope is that the perspectives we have offered will enrich your experience of the meal. We trust that these questions will spark further questions, which will inform our conversation as we eat. Remember, it is in the spirit of Passover to ask questions. There are no wrong answers. The only mistake you can make is to pass up the opportunity to ask, explore, and share. All we ask is that your conversation be informed by the teaching of Jesus at his final seder, "I give you a new commandment, that you love one another. Just as I have loved you, you also should love one another. By this everyone will know that you are my disciples, if you have love for one another" (Jn. 13:34-35).

To that end let us pray: "O, God, teach us to trust you enough to ask the questions we have. Free us from the need to be perceived as clever or informed. Take the elements of the meal and use them to spark our curiosity, open our minds, intrigue our hearts, and deepen our capacity for love. Amen."

קַדֵּשׁ
Kadesh
FIRST CUP OF WINE

[It is customary for the guests to fill each other's glasses and not their own.]

QUESTION

Why do we fill each other's glasses and not our own?

ANSWER

The rabbis teach: What is the difference between heaven and hell? In both, the souls of the departed sit at long tables lavishly prepared with the finest foods. In both, the departed are made to eat with forks too long to allow them to feed themselves. In hell each soul struggles alone to ease a growing hunger. In heaven each soul feeds the soul sitting across the table and in this way all souls are full. Filling each other's glasses brings a taste of heaven to our table; it is a way of welcoming each other and affirming our desire to welcome all humanity to our table-fellowship. It also a reminder of God's commandment to love our neighbor as ourselves (Lev. 19:18; Mt. 19:19).

LEADER

The first cup binds us together in fellowship. We fill each other's cups as we hope to fill each other's hearts. In sharing this drink and meal we remind ourselves of our common bond as children of God.

Ba - ruh a - tah a - do - nai e - lo - hei - nu me - leh ha - o - lam bo -

rei —— p' - ri ha - ga - fen.

COMMUNITY

בָּרוּךְ אַתָּה יְיָ, אֱלֹהֵינוּ מֶלֶךְ הָעוֹלָם,
בּוֹרֵא פְּרִי הַגָּפֶן:

Baruch Ata Adonai Eloheinu melech haolam borai pri hagaphen.

Bless you, Abba, Sovereign of all life, who births the fruit of the vine.

יְרַחַץ
Urchatz
WASHING THE HANDS

[The leader washes his or her hands on behalf of the community as a symbolic act of preparation for leading the community through the seder meal.]

QUESTION
Why do we wash our hands before continuing with our seder?

ANSWER
Washing the hands reminds us that we are entering a sacred space. The rabbis taught that with the destruction of the Temple in Jerusalem and the ending of sacrifice, the dinner table became the new altar, the central place of communing with God. Jesus, too, made Table-Fellowship a central act of his ministry. This banquet, each table around which we sit, is a tabernacle to God. Let us cleanse our hearts and minds even as we cleanse our hands.

כַּרְפַּס
Karpas

BLESSING THE GREEN VEGETABLE

[*Dip the parsley in the saltwater, but do not eat it.*]

QUESTION

Why is the parsley dipped in the saltwater?

ANSWER

Karpas, or green vegetable, symbolizes hope and renewal. The saltwater reminds us of the sweat of the brow, the hard work required if our hopes are to be realized in our lives. The first food we taste at our seder is the food of hope and work.

COMMUNITY

בָּרוּךְ אַתָּה יְיָ, אֱלֹהֵינוּ מֶלֶךְ הָעוֹלָם,
בּוֹרֵא פְּרִי הָאֲדָמָה:

Baruch Ata Adonai Eloheinu ruach haolam borai pri ha-adamah.

Bless you, Abba, Sovereign of all life, who births the fruit of the earth.

[*The karpas is now eaten.*]

Yachatz
BREAKING THE MIDDLE MATZAH

[*One participant at each table, or the leader at the head table, takes the middle of the three pieces of matzah and breaks it in two. Replace the smaller piece between the two unbroken pieces. Wrap the larger piece in a napkin. This will serve as the afikomen, the "dessert." At some point during the seder the afikomen is hidden for the children to find. The afikomen is eaten at the conclusion of the meal.*]

QUESTION
Why do we use three pieces of matzah at our Passover seder?

ANSWER
The number three is sacred in both Judaism and Christianity. For Jews it refers to the three pillars of Judaism: God, Torah and Israel; the three pillars of civilization: wisdom, worship, and love; and the three pillars of human individuality: thought, word, and deed. For Christians, the number three symbolizes the Holy Trinity of Father, Son, and Holy Spirit; and the completeness of God's saving work: the calling out of his special people, the extension of his grace to the Gentiles, and the promise of a new heaven and earth in which his people will dwell.

QUESTION
Why is the middle matzah broken?

ANSWER

For the Jews the broken matzah is the matzah of speech. It is broken because our words are often used to hurt rather than heal and make whole. For Christians the broken matzah is the Son, who died on the cross that we might be saved.

QUESTION

Why do we hide this broken matzah?

ANSWER

There are two reasons. First, we hide half the matzah to remind ourselves how difficult it can be to find the right words to heal the hurts we create in our own and in others' hearts. Second, we hide it in order to remind us to seek God whenever we ourselves are feeling broken and lost. Our hope is that by sharing this meal with each other we begin to find the words of healing and to support each other's search for God.

LEADER

Matzah is called *lachma anya*, the "Bread of Affliction." It is the flat bread of those whose lives have been flattened by suffering and oppression. As you eat this bit of matzah, focus on your God-given kinship with all such men, women, and children. In this way you will awaken thoughts of compassion. Your words will naturally turn toward kindness, and your deeds toward justice.

LEADER

[*Uncover the matzah and lift the plate before the guests.*] This is the bread of suffering, reminding us of the dryness of a soul starved of hope. This is the bread of the broken, reminding us that no one is whole unless all are whole, for in the end we are one body, and when one part of the body aches the entire body suffers.

COMMUNITY

Let all who are hungry share this meal with us. Let all who are enslaved share this meal with us. Let all who are in need share this meal with us. Let all who are in *Mitzraim* share this meal with us.

QUESTION
What does the word *Mitzraim* mean?

ANSWER
Mitzraim is the Hebrew word for Egypt, but it means much more than that. In Hebrew *mitzraim* literally means "the narrow places"; Egypt is symbolic of the narrow places in which we find ourselves enslaved.

QUESTION
Can one who is a Christian be enslaved?

ANSWER
Yes. Jesus said, "You cannot serve God and wealth" (Mt. 6:24), and yet so many of us try to do so. To the extent we serve God we are free; to the extent we serve wealth we are enslaved. There is always a place of enslavement, always a narrow place from which we need to free ourselves. Sharing the bread of enslavement as part of this feast of freedom reminds us that liberation is not once and for all, but is instead an ongoing effort.

QUESTION
How are we to invite all who are hungry to share in this meal?

ANSWER
The call to feed the hungry is a call to action. Our meal is filled with symbols, but it is not itself symbolic. We eat real food and fill real stomachs. At this point in our service, we remind ourselves of the hunger that plagues so many in the world. But it is not enough to remember; we must also act. This is why we were asked to bring canned goods with us to our seder that we might help feed those in need.

QUESTION
Why do we mention both the hungry and the needy?

ANSWER

There is physical hunger and spiritual hunger. Even if our stomachs are filled, our hearts may be empty. This is why Jesus said people shall "not live by bread alone" (Mt. 4:4, quoting Deut. 8:3). How many of us hunger for love, companionship, community, or meaning? Just as we share our food, let us share our hearts as well, taking care to turn our talk to matters of the spirit.

מַגִּיד
Maggid
TELLING THE STORY

THE FOUR QUESTIONS

LEADER

Our seder is a time for asking and answering questions. Four specific questions have been asked for centuries.

READER

How is this night different from other nights?

COMMUNITY

On all other nights we eat leavened or unleavened bread, but tonight we eat only unleavened bread.

READER

Why on this night do we eat bitter herbs?

COMMUNITY

To remind us of the bitterness of slavery.

READER

Why on this night do we dip parsley into saltwater and *matzah* into the *charoset* (apple and nut mixture)?

COMMUNITY

The first reminds us of the bitter taste of slavery. The second reminds us of the sweet taste of freedom.

READER

Why on this night do we eat reclining on a pillow?

ANSWER

In ancient times only the free were allowed to recline at meals. We are relaxed in the company of our friends, eating without fear, and knowing that in this meal all are welcome as they are.

LEADER

O God, we live in a world in which slavery is real and takes many forms. While we may not have experienced political or physical slavery, we confess we have known and know what it means to be imprisoned by poor decisions, unhealthy attachments and dependencies, and sin itself. We remember as well that in Christ you have granted us freedom if only we will accept and use the gift. Tonight help us to know afresh the good taste of freedom and to resolve to live free in you.

THE FOUR QUESTIONERS

LEADER

There are four kinds of questioners: the wise, the foolish, the simple, and the one who knows not what to ask. Each speaks with a different voice: the voices of Wisdom, Doubt, Inquiry, and Faith.

The wise one asks, "What is the meaning of Passover?" This is the Voice of Wisdom that knows our connection with God and seeks to deepen it.

The foolish one asks, "Why do you bother with all of this?" This is the Voice of Doubt that separates us from each other and from God.

The simple one asks, "What do these foods mean, and why do we share them?" This is the Voice of Inquiry that wishes to bring us closer to truth.

The child too young to ask is the Voice of Faith, using silence to invite the telling of our story and the Good News it contains.

THE STORY OF THE EXODUS
[You may choose to shorten the story and sing Let My People Go.]

Let My People Go

When Is-rael was in E-gypt's land, Let my peo-ple go, Op-
press'd so hard they could not stand, Let my peo-ple go.
Go down Mo-ses 'way down to E-gypt's land,—
Tell— old Pha-raoh,——— Let my peo-ple go!

We need not always weep and mourn,
Let my people go.
And wear these slavery chains forlorn,
Let my people go!
Refrain

O let us all from bondage flee,
Let my people go.
And soon may all this world be free,
Let my people go!
Refrain

LEADER

Thousands of years ago a great famine struck the Middle East. Only Egypt had food, for at the counsel of the Hebrew man Joseph, Egypt's Pharaoh had stockpiled food in advance of the famine. He sold the food back to his people and impoverished them. The Egyptians rebelled against this Pharaoh and established a new Pharaoh who enslaved the Hebrew people.

The new Pharaoh feared the Hebrews might lead a revolt against him, and he ordered the midwives to kill all boy babies born to Hebrew mothers. The midwives refused. Pharaoh then ordered his soldiers to raid the Hebrew camps and murder the baby boys.

One Hebrew mother, Yochabed, hid her son in a basket she had turned into a little boat and floated him down the Nile River where he might be found and rescued. She sent the boy's sister, Miriam, to follow the basket to see what became of her brother.

Pharaoh's daughter found the boy. She recognized the baby as a Hebrew, yet her love for life was greater than her fear of Pharaoh, and she raised him as her own son in the Pharaoh's court. Miriam spoke to the princess and offered her mother as a nurse for the boy, whom the princess called Moses. So Moses was raised by two mothers in the House of Pharaoh: the one who gave him life, and the one who saved it.

Being raised as a prince in Egypt, Moses could have turned his back on the fate of the slaves, but his two mothers saw to it that he would not. Both had risked their lives to protect his life, and both would teach him the value of life and the freedom to live it in service to God, compassion, justice, and truth.

One day Moses saw a slave being beaten by a guard. Moses tried to stop the guard and accidentally killed him. Moses hoped the deed would remain secret. When word got out that he had sided with the Hebrew slaves against the Egyptian guards, he fled Egypt to save his life. He ran to Midian where he married Zipporah, the daughter of Jethro, the priest.

Moses was happy in Midian tending Jethro's sheep and raising a family. But God had other plans for the Hebrew prince of Egypt. As Moses was shepherding his flock he saw a bush on fire. He went to investigate and found that the bush burned but was not burned up. God had gotten Moses's attention and spoke to him.

He commanded Moses to return to Egypt and free the slaves. Moses hesitated. He wanted nothing more to do with Egypt and Pharaoh. But in the end he agreed to go, joining with his brother, Aaron, and sister, Miriam, to liberate the slaves.

Moses tried to reason with Pharaoh but was ignored. Pharaoh saw himself as a god and doubted the power of Moses's God. Nine times God brought terrible plagues upon Egypt to convince Pharaoh to free the slaves. But Pharaoh refused. In the end God visited upon Pharaoh and Egypt the same kind of horror Pharaoh had visited upon the Hebrews: the death of the firstborn.

God told Moses to warn the Hebrew people to prepare for liberation. They were to bake flat breads called matzah that could be made quickly and packed in bulk. They were to sacrifice a lamb and smear some of its blood on the doorposts of their homes to mark them as slave quarters. The Angel of Death would pass over these marked houses and spare the firstborn within them. The horror of this plague broke Pharaoh's spirit, and he let the slaves go. But his anger against them rekindled, and he ordered his army to slaughter the Hebrews when they reached the shore of the Red Sea. God parted the waters and the Hebrew people escaped. Pharaoh's army raced after them, but as the last of the Hebrews reached safety, the waters closed about the Egyptians and they drowned.

The ex-slaves rejoiced at the death of their oppressors, but God called to them saying, "How dare you rejoice? The Egyptians are also my children. There is no joy in this. The cost of freedom is high. Respect it always."

In the spirit of compassion for the fallen Egyptians it is customary at every seder to spill out drops of wine for each plague they suffered. In this way we diminish our inappropriate joy at their suffering.

[The plagues are read aloud, and using the pinky of your right hand you remove drops of wine from your cup and sprinkle them on a separate plate or napkin.]

דָּם. צְפַרְדֵּעַ. כִּנִּים. עָרוֹב. דֶּבֶר. שְׁחִין.
בָּרָד. אַרְבֶּה. חֹשֶׁךְ. מַכַּת בְּכוֹרוֹת:

Dahm/Blood	*Tzfardeya*/Frogs	*Kinim*/Lice
Arov/Beasts	*Dever*/Mad Cow	*Sh'chin*/Boils
Barad/Hail	*Arbeh*/Locusts	*Choshech*/Darkness

Makat b'chorot//Death of the First Born

דַּיֵּנוּ:
Dayyenu
IT IS ENOUGH

[Dayyenu—*pronounced* die-ay-nu— *affirms that any gift from God is sufficient and that we do not ask anything from God but that which God desires us to have. The Leader says each verse and the community responds with* dayyenu, *"it is enough." Some groups may prefer to sing the Doxology.*]

LEADER

Dayyenu means "it is enough." We read this to remember all the gifts God gives and to cultivate an attitude of gratitude.

If the Jews escaped from Egypt but the sea had not opened—*Dayyenu*

If the sea had opened but they didn't find manna in the desert—*Dayyenu*

If they found the manna but did not receive the Sabbath—*Dayyenu*

If they received the Sabbath but did not receive the Torah—*Dayyenu*

If they received Torah but not the wisdom to understand her—*Dayyenu*

If they received wisdom but did not receive the Land of Israel—*Dayyenu*

If they received Israel but didn't build the Temple in Jerusalem—*Dayyenu*

If they built the Temple but didn't heed the call of the prophets—*Dayyenu*

LEADER

While it is a good thing to say *dayyenu* and be satisfied with the gifts from God, it is another thing to be satisfied with ourselves. If we wish to be truly free, there is much in our world to which we must say *Lo Dayyenu*, "it is not enough."

If we love ourselves, but not our neighbors—	*Lo Dayyenu*
If we love our neighbors, but not our enemies—	*Lo Dayyenu*
If we end all war, but not starvation—	*Lo Dayyenu*
If we end starvation, but not illiteracy—	*Lo Dayyenu*
If we end illiteracy, but do not protect freedom of speech—	*Lo Dayyenu*
If we protect speech, but do not educate discerning minds—	*Lo Dayyenu*
If we were to educate the mind, but not the heart—	*Lo Dayyenu*
If we were to educate the heart, but not the soul—	*Lo Dayyenu*
If we were to educate the soul, but not the spirit—	*Lo Dayyenu*

THE SECOND CUP OF WINE

[Guests fill each other's cups.]

LEADER

Wine is a symbol of our joy, but it can also be the means of our enslavement. In like fashion, we can become drunk on our own power and intoxicated by the power of others, no longer seeing that only God is Lord. It is for this reason that we preface each cup of wine with a blessing, reminding ourselves to see through the delusion of self-power to the truth of God's power. Jesus said, "[E]veryone who commits sin is a slave to sin," (Jn. 8:34). Our second cup of wine is in honor of freedom. May all who drink it this night move away from sin and slavery toward freedom.

COMMUNITY:

בָּרוּךְ אַתָּה יְיָ, אֱלֹהֵינוּ מֶלֶךְ הָעוֹלָם,
בּוֹרֵא פְּרִי הַגָּפֶן:

Baruch Ata Adonai Eloheinu Melech haOlam borai pri hagaphen.
Bless you, Abba, Sovereign of all life, who births the fruit of the vine.

מוֹצִיא מַצָּה
Motzi Matzah
BLESSING OVER THE MATZAH

LEADER
We are now about to give thanks to God for the matzah and begin the eating of our Passover meal.

QUESTION
What is the significance of matzah?

ANSWER
Matzah is unleavened bread. In ancient times leaven was made from sour dough. Matzah is bread without sourness. During the weeklong observance of Passover, Jews abstain from all leavened products, called *chumetz*. Chumetz symbolizes sourness and the selfishness that causes it. We eat matzah as a reminder to examine our lives that we might stay free from sourness.

The unexamined life is leavened by self-importance, self-righteousness, and self-satisfaction. We honor Passover by seeking to free ourselves from these acts of *chumetz*. Indeed, we Christians may find this focus a natural conclusion to the long season of Lent, with its call to discern and repent of the sins that enslave us to evil.

בָּרוּךְ אַתָּה יְיָ, אֱלֹהֵינוּ מֶלֶךְ הָעוֹלָם,
הַמּוֹצִיא לֶחֶם מִן הָאָרֶץ:

Baruch Ata Adonai Eloheinu Melech haOlam ha motzi lechem min ha-aretz.

Bless you, Abba, Sovereign of all life, through Whom the earth gives rise to bread.

בָּרוּךְ אַתָּה יְיָ, אֱלֹהֵינוּ מֶלֶךְ הָעוֹלָם,
אֲשֶׁר קִדְּשָׁנוּ בְּמִצְוֹתָיו
וְצִוָּנוּ עַל אֲכִילַת מַצָּה:

Baruch Ata Adonai Eloheinu Melech haOlam asher kidshanu b'mitzvotav v'tzivanu al achilat matzah.

Bless you, Abba, Sovereign of all life, who provides us with this opportunity to free ourselves from sourness and selfishness with the eating of this matzah.

[A small piece of matzah is eaten.]

מָרוֹר
Maror
BITTER HERBS

LEADER

It is customary to mix the bitter herbs with the *charoset*, the sweet apple-and-nut mixture. In this way we acknowledge that slavery and freedom go together. We can only know the one in relation to the other. We also remind ourselves that no matter how sweet life may be, there is still the sting of suffering, and that no matter how despairing we may feel or enslaved to habits of the body, heart, and mind, there is always the promise of liberation.

COMMUNITY

בָּרוּךְ אַתָּה יְיָ אֱלֹהֵינוּ מֶלֶךְ הָעוֹלָם,
אֲשֶׁר קִדְּשָׁנוּ בְּמִצְוֹתָיו
וְצִוָּנוּ עַל אֲכִילַת מָרוֹר:

Baruch Ata Adonai Eloheinu Melech haOlam, asher kidshanu b'mitzvotav v'tzivanu al achilat maror.

Bless you Abba, Sovereign of all life, Who provides us with the opportunity to taste the bitterness of slavery that we might struggle for the sweetness of freedom. May the meal we are about to share deepen our friendship with each other and with God. And may this meal be one among many as we labor to reveal the Kingdom of God on earth through the sharing of our food.

[*Make and eat a small sandwich of matzah, maror, and charoset.*]

שֻׁלְחָן עוֹרֵךְ
Shulchan Aruch
DINNER IS SERVED

[As people begin to serve and eat dinner it is wise to remind them that this is a sacred meal, and that conversation should include discussions around the themes of Passover: enslavement and liberation.]

צָפוּן
Tzafon
FINDING THE HIDDEN

LEADER

Earlier in our service we hid the *afikomen*, the broken piece of matzah representing our sense of brokenness and imperfection. Now is the time for us to reclaim what is lost and move toward wholeness. We invite our younger children to hunt for and find the hidden matzah.

Jesus said, "Ask, and it will be given you; search, and you will find; knock, and the door will be opened for you" (Mt. 7:7). While our children hunt for the *afikomen*, ask God for whatever it is you need. Seek out the truth, but don't seek only—find as well. Knock on your own hardened heart that it might be opened to you and to the love of and from God that is God's freely flowing grace.

[*When the afikomen is found, a monetary reward is pledged to a charity of the child's choosing. It is appropriate to let the child announce where she or he wishes the money sent.*]

THE THIRD CUP OF WINE

[*Guests fill each other's cups with wine or grape juice.*]

LEADER

We drank the first cup in honor of fellowship, and the second in honor of freedom. We now drink our third cup in honor of courage: the courage to wage peace as well as war, the courage to reach out with open hands rather than clenched fists, the courage to love not only our friends but our enemies as well. Jesus practiced such courage and calls us to do the same.

QUESTION

We have finished eating. Why add another glass of wine?

ANSWER

There are two reasons. First, our Passover meal satisfied our stomachs, but our souls still yearn for God. The courage to which we pledge ourselves with this third cup of wine is the courage to satisfy not only the needs of the body but also the needs of the soul.

Second, if we fully engaged each other in the spirit of Passover, recognizing our places of enslavement, we may have slipped into another kind of enslavement: prideful and judgmental thinking. We must now free ourselves from those traps and regain the greater solidarity our table fellowship is meant to create. We drink together to reaffirm the importance of people gathering together in God's Name.

COMMUNITY

בָּרוּךְ אַתָּה יְיָ, אֱלֹהֵינוּ מֶלֶךְ הָעוֹלָם,
בּוֹרֵא פְּרִי הַגָּפֶן:

Baruch Ata Adonai Eloheinu Melech haOlam borai pri hagaphen.

Bless you, Abba, Sovereign of all life, who births the fruit of the vine.

ELIJAH'S CUP

[The head table (some communities have a cup at every table) has an empty glass set aside for Elijah, the prophet of peace and herald of the messiah. The glass is passed around as each guest pours some wine into Elijah's cup. The cup is then set in the center of the table.]

LEADER
This is the Cup of Elijah, the prophet of redemption.

QUESTION
Why do we fill Elijah's Cup from our own?

ANSWER
Two thousand years ago Rabbi Naftali introduced this custom saying, "Elijah is the herald of redemption, but we are the vehicles for redemption. Only when we are willing to work for the healing of the world will the prophet come and announce that the time for healing has come."

[The doors of the room are opened to the outdoors, inviting Elijah to join the seder.]

LEADER
"Lo, I will send you the prophet Elijah before the great and terrible day of the LORD comes. He will turn the hearts of parents to their children and the hearts of children to their parents" (Mal. 4:5-6).

As we invite Elijah to our fellowship meal we invite parents to hug their children and children to hug their parents, offering each other the gift of love and forgiveness. As Jesus said, "[I]f you forgive others their trespasses, your heavenly Father will also forgive you; but if you do not forgive others, neither will your Father forgive your trespasses" (Mt. 6:14).

[It is customary to sing a hymn of welcome to Elijah. Any song of healing and reconciliation would be appropriate. While the song is sung, the children are invited to come and watch the Cup of Elijah and see if the prophet does not take a sip from the cup to let all of us know that he is here and the kingdom of God is at hand. The following is the traditional Jewish welcoming of Elijah.]

ELIYAH HANAVI, (THE PROPHET ELIJAH)

Eliyahu ha navi, Eliyahu hatishbi
Eliyahu, Eliyahu, Eliyahu hagiladi
Bim hay rah bi ya maynu, yavo aleinu
im mashiach ben David, im mashiach ben David

Elijah the Prophet, Elijah the Tishbite
Elijah, Elijah, Elijah the herald of redemption.
May the day soon come when the Messiah Son of David is among us.

בָּרֵךְ
Boraych
GRACE AFTER THE MEAL

LEADER

We praise God and give thanks for this fellowship, this meal, and this opportunity to draw closer to God.

COMMUNITY

We praise the Source of Life and devote our lives to enhancing life.

We praise the Source of Justice and devote ourselves to doing justly.

We praise the Source of Kindness and devote ourselves to acting kindly.

We praise the Source of Forgiveness and devote ourselves to forgiving others.

We praise the Source of Hope and promise never to abandon hope.

THE FOURTH CUP OF WINE

[*Guests fill each other's cups with wine or grape juice.*]

LEADER

We drink the fourth and final cup of wine in honor of peace. The Hebrew word for peace is *shalom* from the root *shalem* meaning "wholeness." Peace is not the absence of strife but the ability to engage even an enemy without losing sight of the truth that even one's enemy is part of the human family of God.

QUESTION

King David wrote, "[S]eek peace and pursue it" (Ps. 34:14 NIV). Why did he say both *seek* and *pursue*? What is the difference between these?

ANSWER

The ancient rabbis taught that we are to seek peace when peace seems near at hand, and pursue peace when peace seems far away.

QUESTION

How do we seek peace?

ANSWER

We seek peace when we invite those with whom we struggle to sit at our table and share food and fellowship.

QUESTION

How do we pursue peace?

ANSWER

We pursue peace when we leave the safety of our table and meet the other halfway. We pursue peace when, like Jesus, we go even further and seek out the estranged where they live.

COMMUNITY

בָּרוּךְ אַתָּה יְיָ, אֱלֹהֵינוּ מֶלֶךְ הָעוֹלָם,
בּוֹרֵא פְּרִי הַגָּפֶן:

Baruch Ata Adonai Eloheinu Melech haOlam borai pri hagaphen.

Bless you, Abba, Sovereign of all life, who births the fruit of the vine.

נִרְצָה
Nirtzah
CONCLUSION

LEADER

For thousands of years the Jewish people have remembered and listened to the call of liberation. Tonight we, too, are honored to hear that call.

COMMUNITY

Tonight we remember the bitterness of slavery. Not only the enslavement of the Hebrews to Pharaoh, but our own enslavement to power, greed, and pride; to labels, logos, and manufactured needs; and to sour habits of thought, word, and deed that rob us of dignity and incite us to rob others of the same.

LEADER

Let us stand, join hands and hearts, and honor the call of Passover: the call to accept God's gift of freedom. Let us rise up with courage and grasp hold of freedom that we might fashion a world more strongly committed to justice, kindness, and humility—which was and is the way of the prophets and of Jesus.

COMMUNITY

"Lord, make me an instrument of your peace. Where there is hatred, let me sow peace; where there is injury, let me sow forgiveness; where there is doubt, let me sow faith; where there is despair, let me give hope; where there is darkness, let me give light; where there is sadness, let me give joy"
(Prayer attributed to St. Francis).

FURTHER READING

We recommend the following books to those who would like to learn more about the Jewish Passover seder, its traditions, history, and contemporary use in Judaism.

Women's Passover Companion
Edited by Rabbi Sharon Cohen Anisfeld, Tara Mohr, and Catherine Spector
Jewish Lights Publishing, 2004

Creating Lively Passover Seders: An Interactive Sourcebook of Tales, Texts, and Activities
David Arnow
Jewish Lights Publishing, 2004

The Passover Table: New and Traditional Recipes for Your Seders and the Entire Passover Week
Susan Friedland
Quill, 1994

Make Your Own Passover Seder: A New Approach to Creating a Personal Family Celebration
Alan Abraham Kay, Jo Kay
Jossey-Bass, 2004

Studies on the Haggadah: From the Teachings of Nechama Leibowitz
Nechama Leibowitz,
Urim Publications, 2002

Keeping Passover: Everything You Need to Know to Bring the Ancient Tradition to Life
Ira Steingroot
HarperSanFrancisco, 1995

Passover: The Family Guide to Spiritual Celebration
Dr. Ron Wolfson
Jewish Lights Publishing, 2002

About Paraclete Press

Who We Are

Paraclete Press is an ecumenical publisher of books on Christian spirituality for people of all denominations and backgrounds. We publish books that represent the wide spectrum of Christian belief and practice—from Catholic to Evangelical to liturgical to Orthodox. We market our books primarily through booksellers; we are what is called a "trade" publisher, which means that we like it best when readers buy our books from booksellers, our partners in successfully reaching as wide of an audience as possible.

We are uniquely positioned in the marketplace without connection to large corporation or a conglomerate and with informal relationships to many branches and denominations of faith, rather than a formal relationship to any single one. We focus on publishing a diversity of thoughts and perspectives—the fruit of our diversity as a company.

What We Are Doing

Paraclete Press is publishing books that show the diversity and depth of what it means to be Christian. We publish books that reflect the Christian experience across many cultures, time periods, and houses of worship.

We publish books about spiritual practice, history, ideas, customs and rituals, and books that nourish the vibrant life of the church.

We have several different series of books within Paraclete Press, including the bestselling Living Library series of modernized classic texts, A Voice from the Monastery—giving voice to men and women monastics on what it means to live a spiritual life today, and Many Mansions—for exploring the riches of the world's religious traditions and discovering how other faiths inform Christian thought and practice.

Learn more about us at our website: www.paracletepress.com or call us toll-free at (800) 451-5006.